The Promise Of The Father

Receiving The Baptism Of The Holy Spirit

John J. LoBuglio III

The Promise of The Father

This book is intended as a resource for personal spiritual growth and teaching. It is not a substitute for individual Bible study, prayer, or pastoral leadership.

ISBN: 979-8-218-81397-0

Printed in the United States of America.
First Edition, 2025

DEDICATION

I dedicate this book to the people who have shaped my life and my faith:

To my incredible wife, Amanda, your unwavering love, support, and encouragement have carried me through every season.

To my boys, John, Austin, and Payton, you are my greatest blessings and the legacy I pray to leave behind. May you always walk in the fullness of God's promises and know the power of His Spirit in your own lives.

To my mother, whose recent decision to surrender her life to Jesus and be baptized is one of the greatest miracles I've ever witnessed. You are living proof of God's grace and faithfulness.

To my father, though you have yet to believe, you inspire me every day to be a better example of Christ. I strive to be the witness others were not, praying always that you will one day experience His transforming love.

Finally, to Pastors Gary Toney and Whitman Toland, your investment in my spiritual journey has shaped who I am today in Christ. Your teaching, guidance, and example have deeply impacted my life, and I am forever grateful.

CONTENTS

ACKNOWLEDGMENTS

I want to express my deepest gratitude to everyone who has played a role in my journey of faith and ministry.

To Pastor Gary Toney, thank you for believing in me and giving me the opportunity to serve under your leadership. Your vision for God's kingdom and your investment in people has inspired me more than words can express.

To Pastor Whitman Toland, your wisdom and friendship have been invaluable as I've grown both personally and spiritually. Thank you for challenging me to pursue God's presence above all else.

To my church family at Victory Life, thank you for your prayers, encouragement, and trust. Serving alongside you is one of my greatest honors.

To the many mentors, friends, and co-laborers who have walked with me over the years, you've reminded me that ministry is never a solo journey. Your influence, conversations, and support have shaped not just this book, but my life.

And above all, to my Savior, Jesus Christ. Every word in these pages exists because of You. All glory belongs to You alone.

CHAPTER 1
WHAT IS THE PROMISE

"And behold, I send the Promise of My Father upon you; but tarry in the city of Jerusalem until you are endued with power from on high." Luke 24:49 (NKJV)

Have you ever felt like there's more to your Christian walk, something deeper, more powerful, more purposeful? You're not alone. Jesus Himself promised more. Before He ascended to the right hand of the Father, He left His disciples with a command and a promise.

The command? Wait

The promise? Endued with Power

But let's not mistake this power for mere emotional hype. This is not about an adrenaline rush in a worship service or goosebumps during a sermon. This is the Promise of the Father, the Baptism of the Holy Spirit. A supernatural equipping. A divine enablement to live, walk, and witness like Jesus.

A Note as You Read

Before we go much further, I want to encourage you, don't get caught up on exact wording. You'll see phrases like *baptized in the Spirit*, *filled with the Spirit*, *the Spirit upon*, or *endued with power*. Different backgrounds may use different terms, but they all point to the same life-changing reality: the

Holy Spirit's work in and through you.

The aim of this book isn't to give you a theological dictionary, it's to take a topic that can seem deep or even complicated and make it clear and practical without losing the beauty of what Scripture says.

So, as you read, focus less on the vocabulary and more on the truth behind it. The Holy Spirit Himself will bring the understanding you need.

The Promise is a Person, and the Person is Power

Too many believers stop short. They receive Jesus as Savior, their sins are washed, their name is written in the Book of Life, but they have not yet experienced the fullness of what God has made available. Why? Because they've only encountered the Spirit within, and not upon.

Jesus told the disciples in Acts 1:4-5:

"And being assembled together with them, He commanded them not to depart from Jerusalem, but to wait for the Promise of the Father, "which," He said, "you have heard from Me; [5] for John truly baptized with water, but you shall be baptized with the Holy Spirit not many days from now." Acts 1:4-5 (NKJV)

They already believed. They had seen the risen Christ. Yet Jesus told them to wait. But why? Because belief alone doesn't empower us to boldly proclaim the Gospel in hostile environments. It doesn't produce miracles, or boldness, or spiritual gifts. Only the Holy Spirit does that.

The Power to Witness

Jesus continued:

"But you shall receive power when the Holy Spirit has come upon you; and you shall be witnesses to Me..." Acts 1:8 (NKJV)

The Baptism of the Holy Spirit is not a badge of spiritual superiority; it's the power source for our mission. The early church didn't grow because they had good marketing strategies. It exploded because ordinary men and women were filled with extraordinary power.

Think about Peter. The man who denied Jesus to a servant girl was the same man who stood before thousands at Pentecost and declared Christ with fearless conviction.
What changed? He was filled with the Holy Spirit

This same promise is for you. It's not just for pastors, evangelists, or people in full-time ministry. It's for every believer who wants to walk in the fullness of God's will and purpose.

"For the promise is to you and to your children, and to all who are afar off, as many as the Lord our God will call." Acts 2:39 (NKJV)

The Enemy's Distraction

Satan knows how powerful a Spirit-filled believer is. That's why he's worked overtime to divide the Church on this topic. Arguments, confusion, and fear swirl around the Baptism of the Holy Spirit. But here's the truth: God never gives bad gifts If Jesus said the Father wants to give us the Holy Spirit, why would we hesitate?

"If you then, being evil, know how to give good gifts to your children, how much more will your heavenly Father give the Holy Spirit to those who ask Him!" Luke 11:13 (NKJV)

Let me be clear: the Baptism of the Holy Spirit is not optional if you want to walk in the power of the early Church. It's not an upgrade, it's essential. This promise is the key to a victorious, bold, and fruitful Christian life.

Are You Hungry?

God responds to hunger. He fills the hungry with good things (Luke 1:53). If you're reading this, it's likely because there's a longing in you for more. More than tradition. More than dry religion. More than just surviving until heaven.

You were made for power. You were made for purpose. You were made to carry the Spirit of God, not just in you, but upon you.

This is the promise, and it's waiting for you. From here, we turn to understand who the Holy Spirit is, so we can fully embrace His promise.

Chapter Questions:

1. Why is the Baptism of the Holy Spirit referred to as the Promise of the Father? Does God break His promises?

2. What is your current belief and understanding of the Promise?

3. What connection do you see between the early church's power and their experience with the Holy Spirit?

CHAPTER 2

WHO IS THE HOLY SPIRIT

"And I will pray the Father, and He will give you another Helper, that He may abide with you forever, the Spirit of truth… you know Him, for He dwells with you and will be in you." John 14:16–17 (NKJV)

Before we can understand the Baptism of the Holy Spirit, we must first know the Holy Spirit Himself. Not just as a force. Not merely as power. But as a person. The third Person of the Trinity.

He is not an "it." He is not a cloud, ghost, or a feeling. The Holy Spirit is God.

The Forgotten Member of the Trinity

We talk often about God the Father. We proclaim the name of Jesus, the Son. But when it comes to the Holy Spirit, many believers fall silent, unsure, or uncomfortable. This is one of the enemy's greatest strategies, to reduce the Holy Spirit to mystery, controversy, or fear.

Yet Scripture makes His personhood crystal clear:

- He speaks (Acts 13:2)
- He teaches (John 14:26)
- He leads (Romans 8:14)
- He grieves (Ephesians 4:30)
- He has a will (1 Corinthians 12:11)

These are not attributes of an impersonal force. These are characteristics of a divine person, intelligent, emotional, and active. The Holy Spirit is not distant. He is present and deeply personal.

The Spirit of Jesus

When Jesus walked the earth, He could only be in one place at a time. But He promised something greater:

"It is to your advantage that I go away; for if I do not go away, the Helper will not come to you." John 16:7 (NKJV)

Think about that. Jesus, God in the flesh, said it was better for Him to leave so the Holy Spirit could come. Why? Because through the Spirit, Jesus could live not just with us, but in us.

The Holy Spirit is the very Spirit of Christ (Romans 8:9). He carries the same authority, nature, and purpose. He does not draw attention to Himself but always points to Jesus (John 16:13–14). When we walk with the Spirit, we walk with Jesus.

Not by Might, Nor by Power

We are not called to live the Christian life in our own strength. And we were never expected to. In fact, trying to do so will only lead to frustration, burnout, and compromise.

"Not by might nor by power, but by My Spirit," says the LORD of hosts." Zechariah 4:6 (NKJV)

Many Christians believe in Jesus but live without power. They strive to be holy, to resist sin, to share their faith, but struggle because they are trying to do supernatural things in natural strength.

The Holy Spirit is the Answer.

He is the Helper, paraklētos in the Greek, meaning comforter, advocate, intercessor, strengthener, standby. He's not just beside you; He's in you, empowering you to be who God has called you to be.

The Spirit is God's Presence on Earth

God's work in creation is finished:

"And on the seventh day God ended His work which He had done, and He rested on the seventh day from all His work which He had done." Genesis 2:2 (NKJV)

The Father completed His work of creation and rested. His role in setting the world into motion was done. Then the Son came. Jesus fulfilled His mission to redeem humanity through His death, burial, and resurrection. After this Victory, Scripture records:

"So then, after the Lord had spoken to them, He was received up into heaven, and sat down at the right hand of God." Mark 16:19 (NKJV)

Jesus is now seated at the right hand of the Father. His part of purchasing salvation and restoring the relationship between God and man was completed. Both the Father and the Son are now seated, but the Holy Spirit?

He is not seated
He is active
He is moving
He is in us
He is upon us

The Holy Spirit's work is not done; He is still operating on the earth today. He is the continuing presence of God among His people. He leads, convicts, empowers, transforms, comforts, and testifies. Every supernatural work of God on the earth now flows through Him.

When we ignore the Holy Spirit, we are ignoring the very Person of God who has been sent to walk with us, fill us, and equip us for the days ahead. To live disconnected from the Holy Spirit is to attempt the Christian life without the very One God sent to empower us.

The Spirit of Truth

In a world drowning in deception, compromise, and confusion, the Holy Spirit is our anchor. Jesus called Him the Spirit of Truth. He guides us into truth (John 16:13), reveals the Word of God to us (1 Corinthians 2:10), and convicts us of sin, righteousness, and judgment (John 16:8).

We cannot understand the Word of God apart from the Spirit of God. Here's what's beautiful, He doesn't just reveal truth. He transforms us by it.

"But we all, with unveiled face, beholding as in a mirror the glory of the Lord, are being transformed into the same image from glory to glory, just as by the Spirit of the Lord." 2 Corinthians 3:18 (NKJV)

The more we walk with the Holy Spirit, the more we become like Jesus.

Do You Know Him?

Not just about Him. Not just doctrines and debates. But do you know the Holy Spirit? Do you talk with Him? Do you listen to Him? Have you surrendered your heart to His leading?

Paul ends his letter to the Corinthians with this blessing:
"The grace of the Lord Jesus Christ, and the love of God, and the communion of the Holy Spirit be with you all." 2 Corinthians 13:14 (NKJV)

That word communion means fellowship, intimacy, partnership. This is what you're invited into, a real relationship with the Spirit of God.

This is who He is. Once you know who He is, you'll understand why He came, and why He must not be ignored.

Chapter Questions:

1. How have you previously viewed the Holy Spirit more as a force or as a Person?

2. Why is it important to know the Holy Spirit relationally, not just theologically?

3. How does understanding the Holy Spirit as God change the way you invite Him into your daily life?

CHAPTER 3
THE SPIRIT WITHIN

"Jesus answered, 'Most assuredly, I say to you, unless one is born again, he cannot see the kingdom of God.'" John 3:3 (NKJV)

There is a moment in every true believer's life that changes everything. It's not about joining a church, turning over a new leaf, or adopting a better moral code. It's not about religion. It's about rebirth.

To be born again is to be made new by the Spirit of God. It's the miracle of salvation where death gives way to life, darkness is driven out by light, and a new creation emerges from the ashes of the old.

A New Birth, A New Spirit

Nicodemus, a Pharisee and teacher of the law, was puzzled when Jesus told him he must be born again. "How can a man be born when he is old?" he asked (John 3:4). Jesus' reply cut through all-natural understanding:

"Unless one is born of water and the Spirit, he cannot enter the kingdom of God." John 3:5 (NKJV)

When we surrender our lives to Jesus, the Holy Spirit comes to dwell within us.

- He regenerates us (Titus 3:5).
- He seals us for salvation (Ephesians 1:13).
- He testifies to our spirit that we are now children of God (Romans 8:16).

This is the indwelling of the Spirit, what Jesus meant when He said, "He dwells with you and will be in you" (John 14:17). This is the Spirit within.

The Breath That Gave New Life

"And when He had said this, He breathed on them, and said to them, 'Receive the Holy Spirit.'" John 20:22 (NKJV)

This moment, quietly tucked into the final chapter of John's Gospel, is rich with revelation. It's not merely symbolic. This is the Genesis 2:7 moment of the New Covenant.

Let's go back to the beginning of it all:

"And the Lord God formed man of the dust of the ground, and breathed into his nostrils the breath of life; and man became a living being." Genesis 2:7 (NKJV)

Man's form was complete, but he was not alive until God breathed into him. That divine breath, the ruach (Hebrew- Wind, Breath, Spirit; The breath that animates life), the Spirit, activated Adam. It turned dust into a living soul.

Now fast forward to Jesus, risen from the dead, victorious over sin, and what does He do? He breathes on His disciples and says, "Receive the Holy Spirit."

This was no random gesture. It was intentional creation language. The same breath that gave physical life to Adam was now giving spiritual life to the disciples. This is the moment they were born again.

Before the cross, the disciples believed in Jesus as the Messiah. But the sin debt had not yet been paid. The Spirit could not yet dwell inside them. But now, after the resurrection, the veil was torn. The way was open. And Jesus did what only the second Adam could do, He breathed new life.

This is the Spirit within. It is regeneration. It is salvation. It is the moment the life of God enters the heart of man and makes him a new creation.

Ezekiel's Prophetic Picture

We see this echoed in Ezekiel's vision of the valley of dry bones:

"So I prophesied as He commanded me, and breath came into them, and they lived, and stood upon their feet, an exceedingly great army." Ezekiel 37:10 (NKJV)

Flesh and bone came together. But they were not alive until the breath entered. Then God said:

"I will put My Spirit in you, and you shall live…" Ezekiel 37:14 (NKJV)

Jesus' breath in John 20 was the fulfillment of this prophetic promise. God had always intended to dwell within His people, not just visit them, but abide in them.

This is the reality of being born again. It's not religious reform. It's not behavior modification. It's resurrection from the inside out. You aren't truly alive until the breath of God fills you.

The Spirit Within Marks You

When the Spirit comes to live inside you, everything changes. You go from spiritually dead to spiritually alive. You become the temple of the Holy Spirit (1 Corinthians 6:19). You are no longer just flesh, you are now spirit-born.

"Therefore, if anyone is in Christ, he is a new creation; old things have passed away; behold, all things have become new." 2 Corinthians 5:17 (NKJV)

This inner transformation doesn't mean we never struggle again, but it does mean we now have the power to overcome.

Before Christ, we were slaves to sin. But the Spirit within gives us new desires, a new identity, and a new authority.

You will still face temptation, but now you have a greater power inside you. You may still feel weakness, but that weakness is now the place where His strength is perfected

"And He said to me, "My grace is sufficient for you, for My strength is made perfect in weakness." Therefore most gladly I will rather boast in my infirmities, that the power of Christ may rest upon me." 2 Corinthians 12:9 (NKJV)

Just the Beginning

It's important to understand: the Spirit within is not the same as the Spirit upon. When you are born again, the Holy Spirit comes to live inside you. Jesus described this to the Samaritan woman in John 4:14:

"But whoever drinks of the water that I shall give him will never thirst. But the water that I shall give him will become in him a fountain of water springing up into everlasting life." John 4:14 (NKJV)

This is the *Spirit within*, a well that never runs dry. It is eternal life, springing up from within your spirit. No matter what storms you face, this well is constant. It is the unshakable reality of salvation, God's Spirit taking residence in you forever. But Jesus also spoke of another dimension. In

John 7:38–39, He said:

"He who believes in Me, as the Scripture has said, out of his heart will flow rivers of living water." But this He spoke concerning the Spirit, whom those believing in Him would receive; for the Holy Spirit was not yet given, because Jesus was not yet glorified. John 7:38-39 (NKJV)

Do you see the difference? In John 4, the Spirit within you is a well that springs up into eternal life. In John 7, the Spirit upon you is a river that overflows and touches everything around you.

Salvation is when the well is dug and the water begins to flow. But the Baptism of the Holy Spirit is when that well bursts forth into a river, bringing life, refreshing, and power wherever it goes.

Sadly, many believers stop at the well. They drink deeply of salvation but never experience the river's overflow. But the well was always meant to lead to the river. Jesus offers *both*.

So yes, if you are a believer, you have the Spirit. But the overflowing river, the Spirit upon, is still available. And it's more than a moment. It's a way of life.

Don't Stop at the Starting Line

Far too many believers stop at the new birth. They accept Jesus, are made new, but never step into the full equipping that God offers through the Baptism of the Holy Spirit.

Imagine a runner who trains for a marathon, laces up their shoes, steps up to the start line, and then never moves. That's what it looks like when we settle for the Spirit within but never receive the Spirit upon.

Salvation is your entrance into the kingdom. But there is more. There is fire. There is boldness. There is power. There is a river. There is a promise, and it's time to go after it. The Spirit within is only the beginning. The Father also promised the Spirit upon, which we'll explore next.

Chapter Questions:

1. What does it mean to be "born again" to you?

2. How does the indwelling of the Holy Spirit affect our identity as believers?

3. Read John 20:22, Genesis 2:7, and Ezekiel 37:10-14. What is the significance of Jesus breathing on His disciples?

CHAPTER 4
THE SPIRIT UPON

"But you shall receive power when the Holy Spirit has come upon you; and you shall be witnesses to Me..." Acts 1:8 (NKJV)

If the Spirit within is about salvation and transformation, then the Spirit upon is about mission and empowerment. Jesus never intended His Church to be weak, afraid, or ineffective. He gave us a gift, a supernatural baptism, that enables us to live with boldness, power, and fruitfulness.

This baptism isn't optional for those who want to fulfill the Great Commission. It's essential.

The Promise from the Father

After His resurrection, Jesus told His disciples not to rush ahead into ministry. Instead, He commanded them to wait:

"Behold, I send the Promise of My Father upon you; but tarry in the city of Jerusalem until you are endued with power from on high." Luke 24:49 (NKJV)

Notice that phrase: the Promise of My Father. This wasn't a side gift. This wasn't for a select few. This was the Promise, the fulfillment of prophetic longing, the outpouring foretold by Joel, Ezekiel, and Isaiah. It was the very thing the early believers were told to expect.

"For John truly baptized with water, but you shall be baptized with the Holy Spirit not many days from now." Acts 1:5 (NKJV)

They had already believed in Jesus. They had already received the Holy Spirit within (see John 20:22). But Jesus said there was more. He spoke of another experience, the Spirit coming upon them in power.

Two Distinct Experiences: Breath Then Fire

Jesus breathed on His disciples and said, *"Receive the Holy Spirit"* (John 20:22). They received the Spirit within, the same life Adam received in Eden. It was the divine breath of God entering man again. But then, Jesus tells these same disciples:

"Behold, I send the Promise of My Father upon you; but tarry in the city of Jerusalem until you are endued with power from on high." Luke 24:49 (NKJV)

Wait a minute, hadn't they already received the Spirit? Yes, but that was life. What Jesus is speaking of this is power.

In John 20, Jesus was fulfilling Genesis 2:7. In Acts 2, He would fulfill Joel 2:28: *"I will pour out My Spirit on all flesh..."*

These are not contradictory events. They are complementary. Together, they paint the full picture of salvation and empowerment.

- The Spirit within transforms us into sons and daughters.
- The Spirit upon empowers us to be witnesses and warriors.

When you are born again, the Spirit indwells you. But when you are baptized in the Spirit, He clothes you. It's the difference between the well of water in you and rivers of living water flowing from you (John 7:38–39).

The apostles were born again in John 20, but they were not empowered for ministry until Acts 2.

Breath Starts It, But Fire Sustains It

Don't miss this: the Church began not just with breath, but with fire.

We are born again through the breath of the resurrected Christ and then ignited by the fire of the Holy Spirit.

Both are vital. One gives life. The other gives power.

Some believers have stopped at the breath. They're alive, but not ablaze. They've received the Spirit within, but they've not yet encountered the Spirit upon. And so, they struggle to walk in boldness, to move in the supernatural, to live as effective witnesses. Why? Because Jesus never intended them to stop at John 20. He was leading them toward Acts 2.

Upon, Not Just Within

The language of Scripture is deliberate. The Spirit in us sanctifies and seals. The Spirit upon us empowers.

Throughout the Old Testament, the Holy Spirit would come upon prophets, priests, and kings, giving them boldness, direction, and divine ability. But now, through Jesus, this power wasn't limited to a select few. It was for all believers.

"And it shall come to pass in the last days, says God, that I will pour out of My Spirit on all flesh…" Acts 2:17 (NKJV)

When the Spirit came upon the 120 believers in the upper room (Acts 2), the world was never the same. Timid disciples became fiery apostles. Peter, who had denied Christ days earlier, stood up and preached with conviction, and 3,000 were saved. Why? Because the Spirit had come upon him.

Power to Be Witnesses

Let's be honest: many Christians today live without power. They know Jesus, but they don't walk in boldness. They believe in the resurrection, but they rarely see the supernatural.

Jesus said, "You shall receive power when the Holy Spirit has come upon you; and you shall be witnesses to Me" (Acts 1:8).

Notice the connection: power leads to witness. The Greek word for "witness" is martyrs, the same root for martyr. This is not just about sharing your testimony. It's about living in such supernatural, sacrificial devotion to Christ that your life becomes undeniable evidence of the Kingdom.

The Baptism of the Holy Spirit doesn't just help you talk about Jesus, it helps you live like Jesus.

"He who believes in Me, the works that I do he will do also; and greater works than these he will do…" John 14:12 (NKJV)

Let that sink in. Jesus Himself said we would do greater works, not in our own ability, but by the Holy Spirit.

It's for Today

Some say this baptism was just for the early Church. But Acts 2:39 makes it clear:

"For the promise is to you and to your children, and to all who are afar off, as many as the Lord our God will call." Acts 2:39 (NKJV)

Are you called by God? Are you a follower of Jesus? Then this promise is for you.

This baptism is not reserved for the spiritual elite. It's for every believer who hungers for more. It's not just for pastors or missionaries. It's for mothers raising kingdom children, for teenagers in high schools, for professionals in business meetings. The power of the Holy Spirit is for everyone willing to surrender.

Don't Settle for Less

If the Son of God, sinless, perfect, divine, waited for the Holy Spirit to come upon Him before beginning His public ministry (see Luke 3:22, Luke 4:1,14), how much more do we need this empowerment?

This isn't about emotional hype or spiritual theatrics. This is about heaven equipping earth. This is about divine fire touching human vessels.

The Spirit within saves you. The Spirit upon sends you, and the Church cannot afford to live without either.

Chapter Questions:

1. What's the difference between the Holy Spirit within for salvation and upon for power?

2. Why do you think Jesus told His disciples to wait for the Baptism of the Holy Spirit, even after breathing the Spirit into them?

3. How have you seen the difference between being born of the Spirit and being empowered by the Spirit?

CHAPTER 5

THE BAPTISM WITH EVIDENCE OF SPEAKING IN TONGUES

"And they were all filled with the Holy Spirit and began to speak with other tongues, as the Spirit gave them utterance." Acts 2:4 (NKJV)

There are few topics in the body of Christ more misunderstood, misrepresented, or neglected than the gift of speaking in tongues. And yet, the early Church knew no Christianity without it. The supernatural was normal. The miraculous was expected. And tongues were the initial sign of a believer baptized in the Holy Spirit.

We must return to the standard of Scripture, not settle for the traditions of men.

The Day of Pentecost, The Pattern

Let's begin with what actually happened: Jesus told the disciples to wait in Jerusalem for the "Promise of the Father" (Luke 24:49). They had already received the Spirit within (John 20:22). But now, they would receive the Spirit upon, an anointing of power.

And then it happened:

"Suddenly there came a sound from heaven, as of a rushing mighty wind... Then there appeared to them divided tongues, as of fire... and they were all filled with the Holy Spirit and began to speak with other tongues, as the Spirit gave them utterance." Acts 2:2–4 (NKJV)

Notice the sequence:

1. They were all filled.
2. They began to speak.
3. The Spirit gave them utterance.

Speaking in tongues was not the goal, it was the byproduct. But it was also the first physical evidence of the invisible empowerment they had just received. Tongues are not the Spirit. Tongues are a sign that the Spirit has come upon a believer in power.

The Overflow of the Spirit

Think of it this way: when you fill a glass with water, at some point, it begins to overflow. Speaking in tongues is the overflow. It's the spiritual evidence that you've been filled to the brim and the Spirit is pouring out of your life.

Jesus said:

"He who believes in Me... out of his heart will flow rivers of living water." John 7:38 (NKJV)

John immediately clarifies:

"But this He spoke concerning the Spirit, whom those believing in Him would receive..." (v. 39)

Tongues are not for a select few. They are part of the overflow promised to all who believe.

Tongues: Not the Goal, But a Gateway

Many treat speaking in tongues as the pinnacle of the Christian experience. But that's a mistake. Tongues are not the end, they are a beginning. They are a doorway into a Spirit-empowered life.

Once baptized in the Spirit, with the evidence of tongues, believers are positioned to:

- Operate in the gifts of the Spirit (1 Corinthians 12)
- Pray in the Spirit (Ephesians 6:18)
- Build themselves up in faith (Jude 1:20),
- Speak mysteries to God (1 Corinthians 14:2)
- And intercede beyond their understanding. (Romans 8:26)

Tongues are not weird. They're weaponry. Though it may sound unusual, Scripture consistently portrays tongues as a practical and powerful gift. They are God's supernatural solution for weak human prayer.

Biblical Consistency: Let's take a closer look at the pattern throughout the book of Acts:

1. Acts 2:4 – Day of Pentecost
"They were all filled… and began to speak with other tongues…"

2. Acts 10:44–46 – Cornelius' Household
"The Holy Spirit fell upon all… for they heard them speak with tongues and magnify God."

3. Acts 19:6 – Believers in Ephesus
"When Paul had laid hands on them… they spoke with tongues and prophesied."

This is not a one-time occurrence. It's a consistent pattern: the baptism in the Holy Spirit was always accompanied by the evidence of speaking in tongues.

Why Tongues Are Offending the Mind

Let's be honest: for many, the idea of speaking in an unknown language sounds odd. Why would God choose this? Why not fire from heaven or some other manifestation?

Because speaking in tongues is a test of surrender. It's about yielding the most unruly part of your body, your tongue, to the control of the Holy Spirit.

"No man can tame the tongue. It is an unruly evil…" James 3:8 (NKJV)

The tongue is the most difficult member to surrender. So God chose it as the first sign that a person has been fully yielded to His Spirit. It offends the mind to reveal the heart.

Tongues: More Than One Expression

One reason speaking in tongues is often misunderstood is because many Christians assume it's a one-dimensional experience. But Scripture reveals that "tongues" is a term with many facets, a spiritual gift expressed in multiple ways for different purposes.

Let's look at the three most common expressions:

1. Known Languages (Public Sign)

This is what occurred in Acts 2. The believers were filled with the Holy Spirit and began speaking in tongues, yet foreign Jews from various nations heard the Gospel in their own languages.

"And how is it that we hear, each in our own language in which we were born?... we hear them speaking in our own tongues the wonderful works of God." Acts 2:8,11 (NKJV)

This supernatural moment was a sign to unbelievers, a manifestation of the Spirit confirming the message of the

Gospel in a public setting. Paul later speaks of this use in 1 Corinthians 14:22:

"Therefore tongues are for a sign, not to those who believe but to unbelievers..."

This is not a prayer language, it's a miraculous message in a known human language or understood in their own language, empowered by the Spirit for public witness and evangelism.

2. Spiritual Prayer Language (Private Fellowship)

The second expression is different. This is what Paul refers to when he speaks of praying in the Spirit, speaking mysteries, and edifying oneself. This is not intended to be understood by others, or even by the one praying. It's a personal, intimate language of the spirit.

"For he who speaks in a tongue does not speak to men but to God, for no one understands him; however, in the spirit he speaks mysteries." 1 Corinthians 14:2 (NKJV)

"For if I pray in a tongue, my spirit prays, but my understanding is unfruitful." 1 Corinthians 14:14 (NKJV)

This is what many refer to as a spiritual prayer language, a gift for the believer's personal fellowship, worship, and edification. When you pray in the Spirit, you are:

- Speaking directly to God,
- Declaring mysteries (divine truths),
- Edifying or "building up" your spirit (1 Corinthians 14:4),
- Interceding according to the will of God (Romans 8:26–27),
- And staying strong in faith (Jude 1:20).

This is available to every believer filled with the Spirit, and it becomes a well of continual intimacy and divine empowerment.

3. Tongues with Interpretation (Public Prophecy)

The third expression is when tongues are given publicly in a gathering but are intended to be interpreted for the benefit of the body. In this case, the Spirit enables one believer to speak in tongues, and another (or sometimes the same person) to interpret the meaning by the Spirit.

Paul explains the purpose:
"But he who prophesies speaks edification and exhortation and comfort to men." 1 Corinthians 14:3 (NKJV)

When tongues are given publicly, they must be interpreted so the message can bring edification (building up), exhortation (encouragement), and comfort (reassurance) to the Church. Without interpretation, the Church is not edified, because the meaning would remain hidden.

It's important to understand that overhearing someone praying in tongues during a worship service, prayer meeting, or personal moment is not misuse. That is an individual exercising their private prayer language, engaging personally with God. Public tongues, however, are given with the intent to deliver a message to a group, often with a microphone, platform, or in a way that clearly calls for the Church's attention. Private prayer in tongues strengthens the individual without disrupting corporate order, while public tongues call for interpretation so others may be built up.

Remember in a public setting, when tongues are interpreted, or prophecy is given, the outcome must always be edification, exhortation, and comfort. If a message does not align with these three pillars, it must be weighed carefully. God's voice through the gifts is not harsh, confusing, or condemning, it is uplifting, strengthening, and peace-filled, even when it brings correction.

Paul gave further instruction for how tongues and interpretation should be conducted during a gathering:

"If anyone speaks in a tongue, let there be two or at the most three, each in turn, and let one interpret. But if there is no interpreter, let him keep silent in church, and let him speak to himself and to God."
1 Corinthians 14:27-28 (NKJV)

If a tongue is given publicly without interpretation, it does not edify the body and should be kept private between the speaker and God. God is not the author of confusion but of peace (1 Corinthians 14:33).

The gifts of the Spirit are powerful, but they are never a license for chaos. When operated correctly, they reveal God's heart, demonstrate His glory, and leaves the Church stronger than before.

Tongues, whether in prayer or in prophecy, are tools to bring Heaven's words into the earth. And they are always anchored in love, humility, and order.

What Are You Actually Saying?

Many have asked, "But what am I praying when I pray in tongues?" Paul says you're speaking mysteries to God (1 Corinthians 14:2). These aren't chaotic or meaningless, they're divine truths your mind can't comprehend, but your spirit releases.

Romans 8:26–27 gives even more insight:

"Likewise the Spirit also helps in our weaknesses. For we do not know what we should pray for as we ought, but the Spirit Himself makes intercession for us… according to the will of God."

When you pray in tongues, you're praying perfectly, free from human error, emotion, or ignorance. You are allowing the Holy Spirit to pray through you directly to the Father's heart, bypassing your limitations and aligning with His will.

This is why Paul says:
"I thank my God I speak with tongues more than you all." 1 Corinthians 14:18 (NKJV)

He knew this was not just a momentary sign. It was a lifestyle of divine fellowship, of building himself up for the work ahead, and of praying beyond what his intellect could carry.

It's for You, Today

There's no expiration date on the Baptism of the Holy Spirit. Peter made this clear on the day of Pentecost:

"For the promise is to you and to your children, and to all who are afar off, as many as the Lord our God will call." Acts 2:39 (NKJV)

If the promise is still for today, then so is the evidence.

Tongues are not a denominational badge. They are a spiritual birthright. They don't make you better than others, but they make you better equipped to live in power and pray with precision.

To ignore or downplay speaking in tongues is to overlook one of the most powerful tools God has given the Church. Tongues, as both a public witness and a private prayer language, are part of the Promise.

God didn't design prayer to be limited to human wisdom. He designed it to be supernatural. Tongues allow your spirit to commune with His, to pray with boldness, to war with authority, and to walk with intimacy.

Do I Need to Speak in Tongues?

That's the wrong question. You should ask instead: "Why wouldn't I want every gift and expression the Spirit God has for me?"

Tongues are a beautiful, powerful, and biblical part of the Spirit-filled life. Don't let misunderstanding rob you of divine empowerment. God has more for you, and it begins with surrender. Don't fear it. Don't dismiss it. Receive it, and live empowered.

Chapter Questions:

1. Why do you think speaking in tongues was often the first visible evidence of the Holy Spirit in Acts?

2. What's the difference between known languages (Acts 2) and spiritual prayer language (1 Corinthians 14)?

3. How can you grow in using your spiritual language for personal edification and fellowship with God?

CHAPTER 6
THE GIFTS OF THE SPIRIT

The Holy Spirit does not come empty-handed. When He comes upon a believer, He brings with Him supernatural gifts, tools designed to empower the Church and edify the body of Christ. These are not spiritual accessories or optional add-ons. They are the very manifestations of God's presence operating in and through His people.

The early Church walked in power because it functioned in these gifts. If we want to see that same power in our generation, we must recover our understanding, and practice, of the gifts of the Spirit.

This chapter will explore the purpose, diversity, and operation of the gifts, as well as how they function within the body of Christ.

The Purpose of the Gifts

Paul makes it clear: the gifts are not for personal display but for collective benefit.

"The manifestation of the Spirit is given to each one for the profit of all." 1 Corinthians 12:7 (NKJV)

The gifts of the Holy Spirit are supernatural empowerments given to believers. They aren't personality traits, natural talents, or learned abilities. They are divine capabilities distributed by the Holy Spirit so that we can minister effectively, just as Jesus did.

They are not about platform or prestige. They are about service and stewardship. They are divine solutions to human needs.

The Nine Gifts of the Spirit

Paul outlines nine primary gifts of the Spirit in 1 Corinthians 12. For clarity, we'll group these gifts into three categories: Revelation Gifts, Power Gifts, and Vocal Gifts.

Revelation Gifts - These gifts reveal something that could not be known naturally.

1. Word of Wisdom: A supernatural insight from the Holy Spirit about how to handle a specific situation according to God's will, often involving the future or a divine strategy.

Biblical Example: In Acts 27, Paul tells the men aboard the ship that disaster is coming. Later, he gives divine instructions from an angel about how they can all be saved if they stay aboard the ship. God gave Paul supernatural wisdom to preserve their lives (Acts 27:21–31).

Real-World Example: A believer feels a strong check in their spirit to wait on making a major financial investment. A short time later, the opportunity collapses, saving them from significant financial loss. By following the Word of Wisdom, they have protected what God entrusted to them.

2. Word of Knowledge: A supernatural revelation of specific facts or information that could not have been known naturally.

Biblical Example: In John 4, Jesus tells the Samaritan woman she has had five husbands and is now living with a man who isn't her husband (John 4:17–18). This was a word of knowledge that revealed her situation and opened her heart to the Gospel.

Real-World Example: A believer in a prayer meeting feels prompted to say, "There's someone here struggling with kidney failure, and God wants to heal you." A man confirms the diagnosis, receives prayer, and later reports full recovery. The word of knowledge revealed a hidden need.

3. Discerning of Spirits: The supernatural ability to perceive what is operating in the spiritual realm, whether it is the Holy Spirit, a demonic spirit, or the human spirit.

Biblical Example: In Acts 16:16–18, Paul discerns that a girl following them with flattery is not operating by the Holy Spirit but by a spirit of divination. He commands the spirit to leave her.

Real-World Example: During counseling, a leader senses that a person's torment isn't just emotional, it's spiritual. He discerns a spirit of fear or oppression and prays for deliverance, resulting in freedom.

Power Gifts- These gifts do something; they release God's power into a situation.

4. Gift of Faith: A supernatural surge of confidence in God for a specific situation, empowering a believer to believe for the impossible without wavering.

Biblical Example: Daniel in the lion's den (Daniel 6) is a powerful example. He faced death, trusting God would deliver him. The Spirit gave him supernatural faith to stand firm.

Real-World Example: A missionary is told to leave a dangerous village under threat of death but senses the Lord say to stay. Despite fear, the Spirit gives unwavering faith, and revival breaks out among the villagers who expected him to flee.

5. Gifts of Healings: Supernatural power to heal physical, emotional, or mental sicknesses and restore health.

Biblical Example: Jesus healed countless people, but the apostles did too. In Acts 3, Peter says to a lame man, "In the name of Jesus Christ of Nazareth, rise up and walk." And he does (Acts 3:6–8).

Real-World Example: A believer lays hands on a woman with a terminal illness. She is instantly healed and later receives confirmation from medical tests. The gift of healing flowed through faith and obedience.

6. Working of Miracles: A supernatural intervention by God that defies natural laws, raising the dead, multiplying food, parting seas.

Biblical Example: When Jesus fed the five thousand with five loaves and two fish (John 6:11–13), that was a miracle. The loaves kept multiplying as they were passed out.

Real-World Example: A team delivering supplies to disaster victims runs out of food, but after prayer, more food shows up unexpectedly, sometimes from untraceable sources. God moves miraculously to meet needs.

Vocal Gifts- These gifts say something, they communicate God's will supernaturally.

7. Prophecy: A supernatural message from God, spoken in a known language, that edifies, exhorts, or comforts the hearers (1 Corinthians 14:3).

Biblical Example: Agabus prophesied a famine was coming (Acts 11:28). His prophetic word helped the Church prepare.

Real-World Example: During a service, someone shares a word: "God sees you and hasn't forgotten the promise He made to you." A woman in the crowd begins to cry. She had been asking that exact question in prayer just the night before. God spoke directly to her heart.

8. Different Kinds of Tongues: Speaking in a language unknown to the speaker, either as a sign to unbelievers or in prayer to God.

Biblical Example: In Acts 2, the disciples spoke in known languages they had never learned, declaring the wonders of God to those from other nations (Acts 2:6–11).

Real-World Example: A believer in a prayer service begins speaking in tongues. A visitor from another country understands the words perfectly, it's a declaration of Jesus as Lord in their native tongue. They give their life to Christ.

9. Interpretation of Tongues: The supernatural ability to translate a message spoken in tongues into a known language so the church may be edified.

Biblical Example: Paul says that if someone speaks in tongues publicly, there must be interpretation, so the Church is built up (1 Corinthians 14:27–28).

Real-World Example: During a small group, someone speaks in tongues. Another person, not knowing the language, is prompted to speak the interpretation: "God is calling you to trust Him again." It confirms what several people were sensing in prayer.

Every one of these gifts is powerful, purposeful, and available today. The Holy Spirit distributes them "as He wills" (1 Corinthians 12:11), and yet we are encouraged to desire them (1 Corinthians 14:1). The gifts are not just for public ministry; they are for everyday life. In the grocery store. At the workplace. During your morning prayer. Wherever the Spirit dwells, the gifts can flow.

They are not about spiritual showmanship, they're about manifesting the heart and power of God in real time, in real places, for real people.

Given as the Spirit Wills

One of the greatest misunderstandings about the gifts is that believers must earn them. But Paul clarifies that the Spirit distributes them as He wills (1 Corinthians 12:11).

You cannot manufacture a gift, but you can position yourself to be a vessel through which God flows. Obedience, humility, and hunger are keys.

The gifts are not a reward for maturity, they are tools for ministry. This truth levels the ground, reminding us that God's power flows through availability, not status.

Unity in Diversity

Paul compares the Church to a body: many members, different functions, one Spirit. The gifts are not meant to divide the body, but to unify and strengthen it.

"There are diversities of gifts, but the same Spirit... But now God has set the members, each one of them, in the body just as He pleased." 1 Corinthians 12:4, 18 (NKJV)

A healthy Church honors every gift and every person through whom it flows. Whether prophecy, healing, discernment, or tongues, every gift has value when stewarded in love and order.

The Gifts Require Maturity and Love

In 1 Corinthians 13, Paul reminds us that even the most spectacular gifts are empty if not fueled by love. Gifts may impress people, but love transforms lives.

"Though I speak with the tongues of men and of angels, but have not love, I have become sounding brass or a clanging cymbal." 1 Corinthians 13:1 (NKJV)

The gifts are powerful. But without love, they are dangerous. They must always be submitted to the character of Christ and the nature of the Holy Spirit. Love is the boundary, the motive, and the goal.

Desire the Gifts

Finally, Paul gives a command that many have ignored:

"Pursue love, and desire spiritual gifts, but especially that you may prophesy." 1 Corinthians 14:1 (NKJV)

We are not to fear or reject the gifts. We are to desire them. This is not passive interest, it's passionate pursuit. The Greek word translated "desire" is zēloō, meaning "to burn with zeal" or "to covet earnestly."

In other words, hunger for the supernatural. Long for the power of God. Seek to be used, not for self-promotion, but for the glory of Jesus and the good of His Church.

The gifts of the Spirit are not outdated or optional. They are vital and available. They are tools in the hands of Spirit-filled believers, tools that build, restore, heal, and proclaim the Gospel with power.

We are not called to live with good intentions and human wisdom. We are called to live with the breath of God on our lips and the fire of God in our lives. That means the gifts are not just for the apostles, prophets, or early Church, they are for you.

Ask the Holy Spirit to activate His gifts in you. Seek Him. Yield to Him. But don't stop there, because the gifts weren't meant to run on yesterday's oil. They're meant to flow from a life that stays continually filled.

The apostles didn't just receive power once; they were filled again and again. And so must we. Living the Spirit-filled life isn't about a one-time encounter. It's about daily abiding, drawing fresh strength from the Vine. Let's look next at what it means to "Be Being Filled."

Chapter Questions:

1. Which of the nine gifts of the Spirit (1 Corinthians 12) do you feel drawn to or curious about?

2. How do the gifts build up the Body of Christ when operated in love and humility?

3. Think of a time when you experienced or witnessed one of the gifts at work, in your life or someone else's.

CHAPTER 7
BE BEING FILLED

"Be filled with the Spirit." Ephesians 5:18 (NKJV)

There is a difference between being filled and staying full.

Many believers can point back to a moment when they were powerfully touched by the Holy Spirit. Maybe it was an altar moment, a breakthrough in prayer, or a season of deep intimacy and fire. But then… life happened. Time passed. Trials came. And the fire that once burned so bright slowly dimmed.

This isn't uncommon, and it's exactly why Paul didn't just say, "Be filled" as in a one-time event. In the original Greek, the verb in Ephesians 5:18 is in the present continuous tense, implying an ongoing action. A more accurate rendering would be: "Be being filled with the Spirit" or "Keep on being filled with the Spirit." The Message translation puts it this way "Be filled continually with the Holy Spirit."

Refill Required

Let's be honest: we leak. Disappointments, distractions, dry seasons, and spiritual fatigue all draw from the reservoir within us. If we don't return to the well and refill, even the strongest believer will begin to run on empty.

This is why we can't treat the Baptism of the Holy Spirit as a one-time event; it's the beginning of a Spirit-filled lifestyle. A life where we are continually drawing from His presence and continually renewed in His power.

Filled, and Then Filled Again

Acts 2 wasn't the only time the early Church experienced a filling of the Holy Spirit. Scripture shows multiple moments of fresh filling:

- **Acts 2** They were all filled with the Holy Spirit and began to speak in tongues.
- **Acts 4:8** Peter is "filled with the Holy Spirit" as he addresses the rulers.
- **Acts 4:31** After prayer, "they were all filled with the Holy Spirit" again, and spoke the Word with boldness.

These weren't new salvations or rebaptisms. These were fresh fillings. Moments of empowerment for the moment in front of them. They had been filled, but they kept filling the tank.

Abide To Abound

Jesus explained it this way:

"I am the vine, you are the branches. He who abides in Me, and I in him, bears much fruit; for without Me you can do nothing." John 15:5 (NKJV)

The branch doesn't bear fruit by effort; it bears fruit by connection. It draws life from the vine. The "sap" that flows through the vine is what carries nutrients and power to the branch. That "sap" is a picture of the Holy Spirit, God's empowering presence flowing from Christ to us, through our spirit.

When you abide, you are filled. When you disconnect, you run dry.

Why We Must Stay Filled

1. **Ministry Drains You** Even Jesus had to retreat, and be refreshed. After healing and teaching, He withdrew to secret places to pray (Luke 5:16). If the Son of God needed to refuel, how much more do we?

2. **The World Resists You** We're not living in a neutral environment. The enemy pushes back against the Spirit-filled life. Staying filled equips you to stand strong in a culture of compromise.

3. **The Great Commission Requires It** You can't fulfill a supernatural calling in natural strength. We're called to witness, serve, love, and lead, and we need fresh oil to do it.

How to Stay Full

- **Pray in the Spirit** Jude 1:20 says we build ourselves up by praying in the Holy Ghost.
- **Stay in the Word** The Word and Spirit agree. Let the Spirit breathe on your time in the Word.
- **Worship Daily** True worship fills your spirit as you exalt Jesus above everything else.
- **Walk in Community** Don't do life alone. The Spirit flows through the body of Christ.
- **Obey Quickly** Nothing keeps you sensitive to the Spirit like quick obedience.

Fan the Flame

Paul told Timothy:

"Stir up the gift of God which is in you through the laying on of my hands." 2 Timothy 1:6 (NKJV)

Some translations say "fan into flame." That image is powerful. Fire, left unattended, dies. But when fanned, when fed, when stirred, it burns hotter than ever. You are responsible for your fire.

Don't Be Caught Empty

Jesus told a sobering parable in Matthew 25 that speaks directly to the need for continual filling.

"Then the kingdom of heaven shall be likened to ten virgins who took their lamps and went out to meet the bridegroom. Now five of them were wise, and five were foolish." Matthew 25:1–2 (NKJV)

All ten had lamps. All ten were waiting. All ten started with oil. But only five stayed full.

As the bridegroom delayed, the foolish virgins realized their lamps were going out. They hadn't brought extra oil. They tried to borrow from the wise, but it was too late. And while they ran off to find more, the door was shut.

"And the door was shut... Watch therefore, for you know neither the day nor the hour in which the Son of Man is coming." Matthew 25:10,13 (NKJV)

This parable isn't just about readiness at the end of the age. It's about living full now. The oil represents the presence of the Holy Spirit in our lives, the daily filling, the intentional pursuit of Him, the spiritual discipline of abiding.

The wise virgins didn't have more opportunity; they had more oil. They lived filled.

You Can't Borrow Oil

The most striking part of this parable is when the foolish virgins ask,

"Give us some of your oil," and the wise respond, "No, lest there should not be enough for us and you…" (v. 8–9).

That may sound harsh, but it speaks a powerful truth: you can't borrow someone else's walk with God.

You can't live on your pastor's anointing, your spouse's prayers, or your past experiences. You need your own oil. You need your own fire. You need to keep your lamp trimmed and burning. Living filled is your responsibility.

Stay Awake - Stay Ready - Stay Full

Jesus ends the parable with a charge to watch, to live alert, aware, and awake. In a world trying to lull you to spiritual sleep, staying filled is your greatest defense.

This isn't about fear. It's about faithfulness. It's about being the kind of believer who stays connected, keeps the fire burning, and lives every day ready for His return.

So stir the flame. Stay connected to the Vine. Keep filling the tank. Because when the Bridegroom comes, it's the full lamps that shine the brightest.

In the next chapter, we'll talk about the fruit of that full lamp, the love of Christ flowing from a Spirit-filled life. The greatest evidence of a Spirit-filled life is not just power… but love that reflects the heart of Jesus. Because without love, all the filling in the world is just noise.

Chapter Questions:

1. Read Acts 2, Acts 4, and Acts 13. What do you notice about how often the apostles were filled?

2. What are some signs in your own life that you're running on empty?

3. What daily practices can help you stay connected to the Vine and filled with the Spirit?

CHAPTER 8
WALK IN LOVE

It is possible to move in the gifts of the Holy Spirit and miss the heart of God entirely.

That's not just a theory. It's exactly what the Apostle Paul was warning the church in Corinth about. They had the gifts, but they lacked maturity. They were prophesying, speaking in tongues, seeing healings and miracles, but they were selfish, competitive, and lacking love.

So Paul gives us one of the clearest and most sobering truths in all of Scripture:

"Though I speak with the tongues of men and of angels, but have not love, I have become sounding brass or a clanging cymbal." 1 Corinthians 13:1 (NKJV)

Let that sink in you could operate in heavenly languages… move in great prophetic insight… walk in mountain-moving faith… but if love isn't the motive and the foundation, it's all noise.

Power without love distorts God's intent; love ensures His gifts accomplish their purpose. This is why walking in love is essential to walking in the Spirit.

The Gifts Must Flow Through Love

Paul doesn't pit the gifts against love. He simply says love is what gives the gifts their power and purity.

"Pursue love, and desire spiritual gifts…"1 Corinthians 14:1 (NKJV)

Notice the order: pursue love first. Then desire the gifts. The power of the Spirit and the fruit of the Spirit are never in competition, they are meant to flow together. In fact, the more love fills your heart, the more clearly you can hear and obey the Spirit.

Think about it: Jesus was moved by compassion when He healed, delivered, and raised the dead (Matthew 14:14; Mark 1:41). His power flowed from His love.

Love Keeps Us Grounded

When we experience the supernatural, it's easy to fall into pride or performance. We start measuring ourselves, or others, based on how powerfully they operate.

But love reminds us that the gifts aren't trophies. They're tools, given to serve others.

"But the manifestation of the Spirit is given to each one for the profit of all." 1 Corinthians 12:7 (NKJV)

God gives us His power so that we can build up the body of Christ, not elevate ourselves. Love keeps us grounded in humility, honor, and service.

Love Protects the Integrity of Our Witness

The Holy Spirit empowers us to be witnesses (Acts 1:8). But our character carries our credibility.

We've all seen examples of anointed people whose lack of love, pride, bitterness, jealousy, greed, damaged their testimony. The gifts still worked… but the fruit didn't back it up. And the witness of Christ was wounded.

This is why Paul said:
"Let all that you do be done with love." 1 Corinthians 16:14 (NKJV)

A lifestyle of love validates the power of the Spirit in your life. It makes your message irresistible. It shows the world that this isn't just supernatural power, it's supernatural transformation.

The Fruit of the Spirit Is the Mark of Maturity

The gifts are given. The fruit is grown. You don't mature by performing signs and wonders, you mature by abiding in Jesus and bearing the fruit of the Spirit.

"But the fruit of the Spirit is love, joy, peace, patience, kindness, goodness, faithfulness, gentleness, self-control…" Galatians 5:22–23 (NKJV)

We cannot forget this. The goal of the Christian life is not just power, it's Christlikeness. And the fruit of the Spirit is the nature of Jesus being formed in us. Don't just seek power. Seek to become like Him.

Love is the Greatest

Paul ends his entire discourse on spiritual gifts with this statement:
"Now abide faith, hope, love, these three; but the greatest of these is love." 1 Corinthians 13:13 (NKJV)

Why is love the greatest? Because love is eternal and because God is love.

The gifts will pass away. Tongues will cease. Prophecy will no longer be needed. But love, real, agape, Christlike love, will remain forever.

It's the most powerful force in heaven or on earth. And when the Spirit baptizes you, He not only fills you with power, He fills you with God's love.

Love is a Verb

You were not saved to sit still. You were not filled to be silent.

You've been given the Promise of the Father, the Baptism of the Holy Spirit. You've been empowered, equipped, and anointed to carry the Gospel to the world. To walk in signs and wonders. To speak with boldness. To pray in the Spirit. To manifest the gifts of God wherever you go. But don't ever forget: the Spirit works through love.

"Let your light so shine before men, that they may see your good works and glorify your Father in heaven." Matthew 5:16 (NKJV)

Let your life shine with both power and character. Let the world see a Church full of the Spirit… but even more, full of the love of Jesus. That is the testimony the world is waiting for.

Chapter Questions:

1. Why is love essential to operating in the power of the Spirit?

2. Have you ever seen someone move in spiritual gifts but lack love? What impact did it have?

3. What does it look like in your own life to pursue both the gifts of the Spirit and the fruit of the Spirit?

CHAPTER 9

RECEIVE AND MINISTER THE BAPTISM OF THE HOLY SPIRIT

Jesus never intended the Christian life to be lived in human strength. He told His disciples, "You will receive power when the Holy Spirit has come upon you, and you will be My witnesses…" (Acts 1:8). This power, this supernatural enablement, comes from the Baptism of the Holy Spirit.

This gift is not just for the spiritually elite. It's not earned. It's not reserved for a special few. It is a gift, freely given to all who believe.

"For the promise is to you and to your children, and to all who are afar off, as many as the Lord our God will call." Acts 2:39 (NKJV)

So how do we receive it?

Understand It Is a Gift

Gifts aren't earned; they're received. Jesus said:
"If you then, being evil, know how to give good gifts to your children, how much more will your heavenly Father give the Holy Spirit to those who ask Him!" Luke 11:13 (NKJV)

This is the starting place. The Baptism of the Holy Spirit is not something you work toward, it's something you open your heart to receive, by faith.

Know You Are Born Again

As we've already explored, the Spirit within comes when we're born again, when we place our faith in Jesus and surrender our lives to Him. This is crucial. The Baptism of the Holy Spirit is for believers, those who have already received the new birth.

The apostles received the Spirit within when Jesus breathed on them (John 20:22). But Jesus still told them to wait for the Spirit to come upon them (Acts 1:4–5). Both experiences matter. One is about new life. The other is about divine empowerment.

If you're unsure whether you've received salvation through Jesus Christ, settle that first. Call on His name, surrender your life to Him, and receive the gift of salvation (Romans 10:9–10).

Ask and Expect

Jesus is the One who baptizes us in the Holy Spirit. John the Baptist prophesied, "He will baptize you with the Holy Spirit and fire" (Matthew 3:11). If Jesus is the Baptizer, you can trust His heart. He wants to give this to you even more than you want to receive it.

When you ask, do so with expectancy and faith. *"Therefore I say to you, whatever things you ask when you pray, believe that you receive them, and you will have them." Mark 11:24 (NKJV)*

You don't have to beg. You don't have to wait for a feeling. Ask in faith, believing He gives good gifts to His children.

Release Your Prayer Language

Often, the first manifestation of receiving the Baptism of the Holy Spirit is the ability to speak in tongues, your spiritual prayer language.

"And they were all filled with the Holy Spirit and began to speak with other tongues, as the Spirit gave them utterance." Acts 2:4 (NKJV)

Note this: they began to speak, but the Spirit gave the words. This is a partnership. Many people get stuck here because they wait for the Holy Spirit to move their mouth. But Scripture says, "they began to speak." Your part is to step out in faith and begin speaking, even if the sounds seem strange or unfamiliar. The Spirit will fill your heart and mind with utterances, but you must speak it.

Don't Get Discouraged

Some receive instantly. Others need time. Both are valid experiences. Don't allow doubt, pride, or fear to block your hunger. Keep pressing in. Worship. Pray. Ask. Surrender. The Lord delights in meeting hunger with fullness.

Ministering the Baptism to Others

Once you've received, you can help others receive. In Acts 8:17, Peter and John "laid hands on them, and they received the Holy Spirit." The laying on of hands is a biblical method, but not a formula. The real requirement is faith, both in the minister and in the one receiving.

How to Lead Someone into the Baptism of the Holy Spirit

1. Explain it clearly. Build faith from Scripture.

2. Pray together. Lead them in a prayer like: "Jesus, You are my Lord. I believe the Baptism of the Holy Spirit is Your promise to me. I ask You now, baptize me in the Holy Spirit and fill me with power. I receive it by faith."

3. Lay hands on them (if appropriate) and pray boldly: "In the name of Jesus, be filled with the Holy Spirit. I release the power of God upon you. Receive your prayer language now."

4. Encourage them to speak. Let them know they must open their mouth by faith and begin to speak the utterance the Spirit gives.

5. Stay available. Minister gently. Listen for direction from the Spirit. Be patient, loving, and confident.

You Don't Need a Stage, Just a Willing Heart

You don't need a microphone or a title to receive or minister the Baptism of the Holy Spirit. You just need faith and obedience. Jesus said, "These signs will follow those who believe…" (Mark 16:17). The Baptism is part of the believer's inheritance.

Wherever you go, your kitchen, your workplace, your school, your community, the Spirit goes with you. You are a carrier of God's power.

Now is the time to receive. Now is the time to walk in it. But maybe you've wondered, 'Is this still for me? Is this still for today?' This leads naturally to the question of whether the Spirit is still at work today.

In the next chapter, we'll explore why this promise didn't end with the Apostles, why the gifts and power of the Spirit are still active, and why God wants you to live fully equipped to fulfill the Great Commission."

Chapter Questions:

1. What barriers, mental, spiritual, or emotional, can hinder someone from receiving the Baptism of the Holy Spirit?

2. Why is it important to receive by faith, not by striving?

3. Have you received the Baptism of the Holy Spirit? If so, what changed in your walk with God afterward?

CHAPTER 10

HE IS AVAILABLE TODAY

"For the promise is to you and to your children, and to all who are afar off, as many as the Lord our God will call." Acts 2:39 (NKJV)

The Promise Hasn't Expired

From the day of Pentecost until today, the Holy Spirit has not changed. The power Jesus promised was never meant for one generation, one group of apostles, or one era of church history, it is the inheritance of every believer until Jesus returns.

The promise Peter declared in Acts 2 wasn't limited to the 120 in the upper room. He said it clearly: "For the promise is to you, to your children, and to all who are afar off, as many as the Lord our God will call."

If you've been called by God, this promise is yours. We are still living in the Church Age, the period between Christ's resurrection and His return, and until that day, the Holy Spirit continues to empower His Church.

Even to the End of the Age

Before Jesus ascended, He gave the Great Commission:

"Go therefore and make disciples of all the nations… teaching them to observe all things that I have commanded you; and lo, I am with you always, even to the end of the age." Matthew 28:19-20 (NKJV)

The "end of the age" has not come. That means His presence, His power, and His mission are still active today. The Holy Spirit is still moving. The gifts are still operating. The signs still follow those who believe. The question is, do you believe?

The Enemy's Strategy

In recent years, cessationism, the belief that the gifts of the Spirit ended with the original apostles, has grown louder. It's one of the enemy's greatest strategies: to convince the Church that we're powerless. The enemy knows he is far more effective working from the inside out.

But Jesus knew we couldn't fulfill the Great Commission without His Spirit, His gifts, and His power.

"And these signs will follow those who believe: In My name they will cast out demons; they will speak with new tongues… they will lay hands on the sick, and they will recover." Mark 16:17-18 (NKJV)

This wasn't written as history; it was given as instruction. The signs were never limited to the first-century church. They're for believers, then and now.

Stay Humble and Teachable

Walking in power doesn't mean walking in pride. We must remain teachable, tenderhearted, and dependent on God. The Holy Spirit was given to guide us, not make us self-reliant.

"However, when He, the Spirit of truth, has come, He will guide you into all truth." John 16:13 (NKJV)

God calls us to walk in both power and character. The fruit of the Spirit keeps the gifts in alignment. Love anchors everything we do.

Bringing It All Together

Throughout this journey, we've seen the beautiful unfolding of God's promise:

- **Chapters 1–3** , Salvation brought us the **Spirit within**.
- **Chapters 4–5** , The baptism gave us the **Spirit upon**.
- **Chapters 6–8** , We've been equipped with **gifts**, led by **love**, and empowered for **purpose**.
- **Chapter 9** , We've learned how to receive the baptism and lead others into it.
- **Chapter 10** , Now we stand in this truth: **the Promise is still for today**.

This isn't just a theology to believe, it's an invitation to experience His fullness.

The Final Call

The same Holy Spirit who transformed Peter, Paul, and the early church is still available. He has not stopped filling, empowering, healing, and sending believers into the world.

The world needs Spirit-filled Christians now more than ever, believers who carry the power of God and the love of Christ into their workplaces, schools, neighborhoods, and nations. The Promise is still alive. The gifts are still active. The mission is still urgent. And you are called to be part of it.

"Be filled with the Spirit." Ephesians 5:18 (NKJV)

This call echoes through every generation—yours and mine included.

Chapter Questions:

1. Acts 2:39 says the promise of the Holy Spirit is "to you… and all who are afar off." How does knowing this promise is for you today impact your faith and expectations?

2. Why do you think the enemy works so hard to convince believers that the gifts of the Spirit and the baptism of power are no longer for today? What scriptures strengthen your confidence that the promise is still available?

3. Jesus said, "You shall receive power when the Holy Spirit has come upon you… and you shall be My witnesses" Acts 1:8. In what specific areas of your life is God calling you to step out in Spirit empowered boldness

The Promise Of The Father

21 Day Devotional

Introduction to the 21-Day Devotional

The journey of following Jesus was never meant to be lived in our own strength. From the very beginning, God promised His Spirit would dwell within us and rest upon us to empower us for life, transformation, and His mission. This 21-day devotional is designed to help you experience more of God's presence, deepen your understanding of the Holy Spirit, and walk boldly in the power He has made available to every believer.

Each day includes a devotional reading, scripture focus, reflection questions, and a Secret Place Moment where you are invited to pause, pray, and listen to the Holy Spirit. This isn't meant to be rushed or treated as another checklist item, it's an invitation to slow down, spend time in God's presence, and let His Spirit transform your heart.

Take it one day at a time. Read the devotional thoughtfully, meditate on the scriptures, and allow the questions to guide your personal reflection or group discussion. Most importantly, invite the Holy Spirit to speak to you and respond to His leading.

By the end of these 21 days, my prayer is that you'll walk in deeper intimacy with God, a greater awareness of His Spirit, and renewed confidence in His power working through you.

Day 1 — The Father's Promise

Scripture Focus:

Acts 1:4-5, Joel 2:28-29, Luke 24:49

Devotional

Before ascending into heaven, Jesus gave His disciples one clear instruction: wait. He told them, "Do not leave Jerusalem, but wait for the Promise of the Father, which you have heard from Me; for John truly baptized with water, but you shall be baptized with the Holy Spirit not many days from now" (Acts 1:4-5).

This was not a suggestion, it was a command. Jesus knew that fulfilling the Great Commission would require more than human effort, they needed supernatural empowerment. The prophet Joel had spoken of this moment centuries earlier, saying, "I will pour out My Spirit on all flesh" (Joel 2:28).

Jesus confirmed God's plan in Luke 24:49: "Behold, I send the Promise of My Father upon you; but stay in the city until you are clothed with power from on high." That same power is available to you today. The Baptism of the Holy Spirit is not reserved for a select few, it is God's gift to every believer.

Without His Spirit, we strive in our own strength. With Him, we are empowered to live boldly, love deeply, and fulfill God's calling on our lives. The Father's promise still stands, and He desires to fill you afresh.

Reflection Questions

1. How does understanding this promise in both the Old and New Testaments strengthen your faith?

____

____

____

2. Where in your life do you need the Spirit's empowerment most?

____

____

____

3. Are there fears or misconceptions keeping you from receiving more of God's Spirit?

____

____

____

Secret Place Moment

Set aside 10 minutes today to read Acts 1:4-8 and Joel 2:28-29 slowly. Invite the Holy Spirit to increase your hunger for Him.

Pray: "Holy Spirit, I want everything You have for me. Fill me today and empower me to walk in boldness."

Day 2 — The Spirit Within

Scripture Focus:

John 4:14, Ezekiel 36:26-27, Romans 8:9

Devotional

When you surrendered your life to Christ, the Holy Spirit came to dwell within you. Jesus said, "Whoever drinks the water I give them will never thirst. Indeed, the water I give them will become in them a spring of water welling up to eternal life" (John 4:14). The Spirit is not distant, He resides in your heart, guiding you, renewing you, and transforming you into the image of Christ.

Centuries earlier, God promised, "I will give you a new heart and put a new spirit within you" (Ezekiel 36:26). Through salvation, that promise became reality. His presence within you is evidence of your adoption into His family and a reminder that you are never alone. Romans 8:9 declares, "If anyone does not have the Spirit of Christ, they do not belong to Christ."

Living with the Spirit within means you no longer depend on your own strength. He produces fruit in your life, convicts you when you wander, and equips you to walk in freedom. The Spirit within is God's personal guarantee that you are His, and He is committed to shaping your heart to reflect His nature.

Reflection Questions

1. How does knowing the Holy Spirit lives within you change the way you see yourself?

____

____

____

2. What areas of your life need His transforming power?

____

____

____

3. How can you become more aware of His presence in your daily decisions?

____

____

____

Secret Place Moment

Find a quiet place today, close your eyes, and simply acknowledge the Holy Spirit's presence within you.

Pray: "Holy Spirit, thank You for living in me. Teach me to listen to Your voice and walk closely with You each day."

Day 3 — The Spirit Upon

Scripture Focus:

Acts 1:8, Isaiah 61:1, Judges 6:34

Devotional

Jesus promised, "You will receive power when the Holy Spirit has come upon you, and you will be My witnesses" (Acts 1:8). The Spirit within transforms your character, but the Spirit upon equips you for God's mission.

Isaiah declared, "The Spirit of the Lord is upon Me, because He has anointed Me to proclaim good news to the poor" (Isaiah 61:1). When Gideon faced impossible odds, Judges 6:34 says "the Spirit of the Lord came upon him," empowering him for victory. Similarly, in Acts, ordinary believers were transformed into bold witnesses when the Spirit came upon them.

This empowerment is not limited to history; it is available today. God's Spirit equips you with boldness, wisdom, and supernatural ability to fulfill your calling. It's not about relying on natural strength but about yielding to His power.

If you've been saved but feel unequipped, the baptism of the Spirit is God's gift for you. He desires to clothe you with power so you can live courageously, love deeply, and make a lasting impact on those around you.

Reflection Questions

1. What is the difference between the Spirit within and the Spirit upon?

____

____

____

2. Where in your life do you need God's empowerment?

____

____

____

3. How can you position yourself to be used more fully by Him?

____

____

____

Secret Place Moment

Ask God to clothe you with His power today.

Pray: "Father, I surrender to You. Let Your Spirit come upon me and empower me to do what I cannot do on my own."

Day 4 — Receiving the Baptism

Scripture Focus:

Luke 11:13, Acts 2:1-4, John 7:37-39

Devotional

The Baptism of the Holy Spirit is a promise for every believer. Jesus said, "How much more will your Father in heaven give the Holy Spirit to those who ask Him" (Luke 11:13). God's desire is for you to be filled and empowered to live the life He has called you to.

On the day of Pentecost, the disciples simply waited, prayed, and received (Acts 2:1-4). They didn't strive for it; they positioned their hearts with expectancy and allowed God to move. In John 7:37-39, Jesus described the Spirit as "rivers of living water" flowing from within believers, refreshing and empowering them.

Receiving the baptism comes by faith, not effort. You don't have to earn it; you simply believe and yield. God desires to pour out His Spirit upon you so you can walk in confidence and strength.

Ask boldly, trust fully, and expect God to fill you. The same Spirit who empowered the early Church is ready to empower you today.

Reflection Questions

1. What thoughts or fears have kept you from fully receiving God's promise?

____

____

____

2. How does knowing the Father desires to give you His Spirit change your approach to prayer?

____

____

____

3. Are you expecting God to move in your life, or settling for less than He promised?

____

____

____

Secret Place Moment

Set aside time today to pray boldly and expectantly. Ask the Father to fill you afresh with His Spirit.

Pray: "Father, I receive Your promise by faith. Fill me with Your Spirit and let Your power flow through me."

Day 5 — Tongues: A Gift for You

Scripture Focus:

Mark 16:17, Acts 2:4, 1 Corinthians 14:2

Devotional

Jesus said, "These signs will follow those who believe… they will speak in new tongues" (Mark 16:17). On the day of Pentecost, "they were all filled with the Holy Spirit and began to speak in other tongues as the Spirit enabled them" (Acts 2:4).

Speaking in tongues is a beautiful gift given by God to every Spirit-filled believer. It strengthens your faith, deepens your intimacy with Him, and allows you to pray beyond your understanding. Paul explains, "Anyone who speaks in a tongue does not speak to people but to God… they utter mysteries by the Spirit" (1 Corinthians 14:2).

Praying in the Spirit aligns your heart with God's will and builds up your inner man. It's not reserved for a select few, it's for all who believe and receive.

God desires for you to experience the fullness of this gift. Ask Him to activate it in your life and let His Spirit lead you into deeper prayer and worship.

Reflection Questions

1. What comes to mind when you think about praying in tongues?

____

____

____

2. How could this gift strengthen your prayer life?

____

____

____

3. Are you open to receiving all God has for you, even if it stretches your understanding?

____

____

____

Secret Place Moment

Spend time today inviting the Holy Spirit to activate His gifts within you.

Pray: "Holy Spirit, I desire every gift You have for me. Help me pray Your perfect will and draw closer to You."

Day 6 — Gifts of the Spirit

Scripture Focus:

1 Corinthians 12:7-11, Romans 12:6-8, 1 Peter 4:10

Devotional

Paul writes, "To each one the manifestation of the Spirit is given for the common good" (1 Corinthians 12:7). Spiritual gifts are given by God so the Body of Christ can thrive. These gifts, wisdom, healing, prophecy, discernment, and others; are unique expressions of His power working through you.

Romans 12 reminds us that gifts differ, but each one is essential. 1 Peter 4:10 calls us to "use whatever gift you have received to serve others, as faithful stewards of God's grace." God gives you gifts not for your glory but to build His Kingdom and bless others.

Discovering your gifts begins with prayer and willingness. As you step out in faith, God reveals and develops what He has placed within you.

Don't bury your gift, use it. As you grow in obedience, God will multiply your impact for His glory.

Reflection Questions

1. Which spiritual gifts do you feel drawn to or already see operating in your life?

2. How can you use your gifts to serve others more intentionally?

3. What is one step you can take this week to develop your God given gifts?

Secret Place Moment

Ask God to reveal and develop the gifts He has placed within you.

Pray: "Father, thank You for the gifts of Your Spirit. Show me how to use them to serve others and glorify You."

Day 7 — Walk in Love

Scripture Focus:

1 Corinthians 13:1-3, Galatians 5:22-23, John 13:34

Devotional

Paul reminds us, "If I speak in the tongues of men or of angels but do not have love, I am only a resounding gong or a clanging cymbal" (1 Corinthians 13:1). Love is the foundation of the Spirit-filled life. Without it, even the most powerful gifts lose their meaning.

Jesus said, "Love one another as I have loved you" (John 13:34). Love is also the first fruit of the Spirit listed in Galatians 5:22, showing us that genuine spiritual maturity flows from a heart transformed by God's love.

Spiritual gifts operate best when motivated by compassion. Love turns ministry from duty into delight and draws people to Christ. When we walk in love, we reflect God's nature and give life to the gifts He's entrusted to us.

Choose today to lead with love. Let every action, word, and gift point people to Jesus.

Reflection Questions

1. How does love shape the way you use your spiritual gifts?

____

____

____

2. Who in your life needs to see God's love expressed through you?

____

____

____

3. How can you grow in demonstrating love daily?

____

____

____

Secret Place Moment

Take time today to sit with God and ask Him to fill you with His love for others.

Pray: "Lord, help me walk in Your love and let everything I do point others to You."

Day 8 — Empowered to Witness

Scripture Focus:

Matthew 28:18-20, Acts 4:31, Romans 1:16

Devotional

Jesus gave us a clear mission: "Go and make disciples of all nations" (Matthew 28:19). But He never intended for us to fulfill that mission in our own strength. Before ascending, He promised the Holy Spirit so that we could live boldly and speak with power.

Acts 4:31 shows that after the believers prayed, "they were all filled with the Holy Spirit and spoke the word of God boldly." The Spirit transforms fear into faith and timidity into confidence. Through Him, your words carry eternal weight.

Romans 1:16 reminds us, "I am not ashamed of the gospel, because it is the power of God that brings salvation to everyone who believes." Evangelism isn't about eloquence or persuasion; it's about allowing the Spirit to work through you.

When you're filled with the Spirit, sharing your faith becomes an overflow of God's love within you. You don't have to force it; the Spirit empowers you to witness naturally and effectively.

Reflection Questions

1. How does the Spirit's empowerment change your view of sharing the Gospel?

____

____

____

2. Who in your life needs to hear about Jesus today?

____

____

____

3. What fears hold you back from being a bold witness?

____

____

____

Secret Place Moment

Pray for boldness to share Jesus with someone in your life. Ask the Spirit to open doors and give you the right words.

Pray: "Holy Spirit, fill me with boldness and lead me to those who need Your love."

Day 9 — Living on Mission

Scripture Focus:

Acts 13:2-3, Isaiah 6:8, John 20:21

Devotional

God saved you with purpose. In Acts 13:2, the Spirit said, "Set apart for Me Barnabas and Saul for the work to which I have called them." Like them, you've been set apart to fulfill God's plan for your life.

Isaiah responded to God's call saying, "Here am I. Send me!" (Isaiah 6:8). That same willingness positions you to walk in your assignment. Jesus echoed this truth in John 20:21: "As the Father has sent Me, I am sending you."

Living on mission doesn't mean becoming a pastor or missionary unless God calls you there. It means surrendering daily, seeking His will, and impacting the people in front of you. The Spirit equips you for every encounter, at home, at work, and in your community.

Your greatest influence often flows from ordinary faithfulness. When you live Spirit-led, God uses your life as a beacon to draw others to Him.

Reflection Questions

1. What does it mean to you to live on mission daily?

____

____

____

2. Where has God already placed opportunities for you to influence others?

____

____

____

3. Are you willing to be set apart for His purposes?

____

____

____

Secret Place Moment

Ask God to open your heart to His daily assignments and how you can prepare for them.

Pray: "Lord, I surrender my plans to You. Send me wherever You want me to go."

Day 10 — Signs That Follow

Scripture Focus:

Mark 16:17-18, Acts 5:12-16, Hebrews 2:4

Devotional

Jesus said, "These signs will follow those who believe" (Mark 16:17). The early church experienced miracles regularly; Acts 5:12 says, "The apostles performed many signs and wonders among the people." God confirmed His Word with demonstrations of His power.

Hebrews 2:4 reminds us that God "testified to it by signs, wonders, and various miracles, and by gifts of the Holy Spirit." These signs weren't for show; they pointed people to Jesus and revealed His Kingdom breaking into the earth.

The same Spirit who moved in Acts still works today. Signs and wonders are evidence of God's love, not proof of our strength. They follow belief, not the other way around.

When you step out in faith, God shows Himself faithful. Be bold enough to pray for the impossible and trust that His power is still at work through you.

Reflection Questions

1. How do you view signs and wonders today?

____

____

____

2. What might God want to reveal about His power through you?

____

____

____

3. Are you willing to step out in faith and pray for the impossible?

____

____

____

Secret Place Moment

Pray boldly for God's power to be demonstrated in your life for His glory.

Pray: "Holy Spirit, work through me to reveal Jesus to others. Use me to demonstrate Your love and power."

Day 11 — Tongues: A Weapon

Scripture Focus:

Ephesians 6:18, Romans 8:26, Isaiah 28:11-12

Devotional

Praying in tongues isn't just a gift; it's a spiritual weapon. Ephesians 6:18 calls us to "pray in the Spirit on all occasions with all kinds of prayers and requests." Tongues unlock a direct connection between your spirit and God's.

Romans 8:26 says, "The Spirit Himself intercedes for us through wordless groans." When you don't know how to pray, the Spirit prays perfectly on your behalf, aligning you with God's will. Isaiah 28:11-12 even describes tongues as a place of "rest" and "refreshing" for God's people.

Praying in the Spirit builds your faith, strengthens your inner man, and brings supernatural clarity when your mind feels overwhelmed. It shifts atmospheres, intercedes for needs you can't see, and prepares the way for breakthrough.

Use this weapon daily. The Spirit knows the heart of the Father better than we ever could, and when you yield your tongue, you step into heavenly partnership.

Reflection Questions

1. How often do you pray in the Spirit?

____

____

____

2. What would change if you began using this gift daily?

____

____

____

3. How does praying in tongues strengthen you spiritually?

____

____

____

Secret Place Moment

Spend 5 to 10 minutes today praying in the Spirit, letting Him guide your prayers.

Pray: "Holy Spirit, help me pray Your will when my words fall short. Strengthen my spirit today."

Day 12 — The Nine Gifts

Scripture Focus:

1 Corinthians 12:7-11, Romans 12:6-8, 1 Peter 4:10

Devotional

Paul outlines nine spiritual gifts in 1 Corinthians 12, given for the benefit of all. These include wisdom, knowledge, faith, healing, miracles, prophecy, discernment, tongues, and interpretation. Each gift is an expression of God's power and grace flowing through His people.

Romans 12 reminds us that these gifts differ, but all are essential. 1 Peter 4:10 calls us to "use whatever gift you have received to serve others, as faithful stewards of God's grace." The gifts are not for status or recognition but to reveal God's heart and build His Kingdom.

Discovering your gifts begins with prayer, study, and stepping out in faith. As you obey God's leading, He'll reveal how He wants to use you.

Every believer is uniquely equipped. Your gifts matter. Don't bury them; embrace them and use them to point others to Jesus.

Reflection Questions

1. Which of the nine gifts do you feel drawn toward?

____

____

____

2. How can you better develop and activate those gifts?

____

____

____

3. Who in your life could benefit from you operating in your gifts?

____

____

____

Secret Place Moment

Ask the Lord to reveal which gifts He has placed in you and how He wants you to use them.

Pray: "Father, I desire to steward the gifts You have entrusted to me. Use me to serve others and glorify You."

Day 13 — Discovering Your Gift

Scripture Focus:

1 Corinthians 12:27-31, Ephesians 4:11-13, Matthew 25:14-30

Devotional

You were uniquely created by God and equipped with gifts that serve His Kingdom. 1 Corinthians 12:27 says, "Now you are the body of Christ, and each one of you is a part of it." Every believer plays a vital role, and your gifts matter deeply.

Ephesians 4:11-13 explains that God gave different roles and abilities to build up the Church. Your gifting may not look like someone else's, and that's the beauty of the Body of Christ. God intentionally designed you to bring something unique to the table.

In Matthew 25, Jesus tells the parable of the talents, teaching us that we are responsible for stewarding what God has entrusted to us. Your gifts aren't meant to stay hidden; they grow when you put them to use.

Ask God to reveal your giftings and show you where to serve. As you step out in faith, He'll develop and strengthen the gifts He's placed inside you for His glory.

Reflection Questions

1. What gifts has God already revealed in your life?

____

____

____

2. How can you start using your gifts more intentionally this week?

____

____

____

3. Are there areas where fear has kept you from stepping out?

____

____

____

Secret Place Moment

Ask God to give you clarity about your role in His Kingdom and boldness to step into it.

Pray: "Lord, reveal the gifts You have given me and show me how to use them for Your glory."

Day 14 — The Greatest Gift: Love

Scripture Focus:

1 Corinthians 13:1-3, John 13:34-35, Galatians 5:22

Devotional

Paul reminds us in 1 Corinthians 13 that without love, even the most powerful gifts lose their meaning: "If I have the gift of prophecy and can fathom all mysteries and all knowledge, but do not have love, I am nothing" (v.2). Spiritual gifts are incredible tools for advancing God's Kingdom, but love is the foundation they must rest on.

Jesus said, "By this everyone will know that you are My disciples, if you love one another" (John 13:35). Love is the evidence that we belong to Him, and it is the first fruit of the Spirit listed in Galatians 5:22. A Spirit-filled life cannot be separated from a life of genuine love.

True ministry flows from compassion. The gifts of the Spirit are meant to serve people, not impress them. When love motivates us, our words carry weight, our actions reveal Christ, and our gifts operate with greater effectiveness. Without love, we risk drawing attention to ourselves rather than pointing people to Jesus.

Walking in love requires choosing patience, kindness, humility, and forgiveness daily. As we remain connected to God's heart, His love flows naturally through us to others.

Reflection Questions

1. How do you prioritize love when using your gifts?

____

____

____

2. Who needs to experience God's love through you today?

____

____

____

3. What can you do to cultivate a greater love for others?

____

____

____

Secret Place Moment

Ask God to fill your heart with His love until it overflows to those around you.

Pray: "Holy Spirit, fill me with Your love and teach me to reflect Your heart in everything I do."

Day 15 — Walking in the Fruit

Scripture Focus:

Galatians 5:22-23, John 15:5, Colossians 3:12-14

Devotional

The gifts of the Spirit demonstrate God's power, but the fruit of the Spirit reveals His nature. Galatians 5:22-23 lists love, joy, peace, patience, kindness, goodness, faithfulness, gentleness, and self-control as evidence of a Spirit-led life.

Jesus said, "I am the vine; you are the branches. If you remain in Me and I in you, you will bear much fruit" (John 15:5). The key to fruitfulness is staying connected to Him through prayer, worship, and His Word. As you remain close to God, His Spirit produces lasting change from the inside out.

Colossians 3:14 reminds us to "put on love, which binds them all together in perfect unity." The fruit of the Spirit keeps us rooted in Christ's character and allows us to represent Him well to the world.

Spiritual maturity is measured not by power but by love, humility, and transformation. Stay connected to the Vine, and fruit will flourish naturally.

Reflection Questions

1. Which fruit of the Spirit do you see growing strongest in your life?

____

____

____

2. Which one do you most want God to develop further?

____

____

____

3. How can you stay better connected to the vine each day?

____

____

____

Secret Place Moment

Ask God to produce His fruit in your heart and help you stay rooted in Him.

Pray: "Holy Spirit, shape my character to reflect Jesus more each day."

Day 16 — Empowered to Witness

Scripture Focus:

Acts 4:31, Matthew 5:14-16, Romans 1:16

Devotional

The Baptism of the Holy Spirit isn't only for personal growth; it equips you for God's mission. In Acts 4:31, "they were all filled with the Holy Spirit, and they spoke the word of God boldly." The Spirit turns ordinary believers into courageous witnesses.

Jesus said, "You are the light of the world. A city set on a hill cannot be hidden" (Matthew 5:14). Your calling is to shine His light wherever you go. The Spirit gives you wisdom, courage, and supernatural opportunities to share your faith in ways that impact hearts.

Romans 1:16 declares, "I am not ashamed of the gospel, for it is the power of God that brings salvation to everyone who believes." The same Spirit who empowered the early Church empowers you to share Jesus effectively.

When you yield to the Spirit's leading, evangelism becomes less about striving and more about overflow. God speaks through willing vessels; you just have to say yes.

Reflection Questions

1. How confident are you in sharing your faith?

___

___

___

2. What fears have held you back from witnessing before?

___

___

___

3. Who in your life needs to hear the Gospel today?

___

___

___

Secret Place Moment

Ask the Spirit to give you boldness and divine opportunities to share Jesus.

Pray: "Holy Spirit, empower me to be Your witness and shine Your light wherever I go."

Day 17 — Living Spirit Led

Scripture Focus:

Romans 8:14, Galatians 5:25, Isaiah 30:21

Devotional

To be Spirit-filled is to be Spirit-led. Romans 8:14 says, "Those who are led by the Spirit of God are the children of God." The Holy Spirit desires to guide your steps daily, leading you into God's will and away from unnecessary struggles.

Galatians 5:25 says, "Since we live by the Spirit, let us keep in step with the Spirit." Living Spirit-led means choosing His voice over fear, doubt, and distractions. Isaiah 30:21 promises, "Your ears will hear a voice behind you saying, 'This is the way; walk in it.'"

The Spirit directs, teaches, and warns; but He leads those who listen. When you slow down to seek His guidance, you'll find clarity and confidence in your decisions.

A Spirit-led life isn't complicated; it's about relationship. As you lean into His presence, you'll find peace, direction, and supernatural alignment with God's plan.

Reflection Questions

1. How can you become more sensitive to the Holy Spirit's leading?

____

____

____

2. What distractions keep you from hearing His voice clearly?

____

____

____

3. What is one area of your life where you need His direction right now?

____

____

____

Secret Place Moment

Ask the Holy Spirit to speak to you today about one decision you are facing.

Pray: "Holy Spirit, lead me in every step I take and guide me into Your perfect will."

Day 18 — Helping Others Receive

Scripture Focus:

Acts 8:14-17, Acts 19:1-6, Galatians 3:14

Devotional

The Baptism of the Holy Spirit isn't just for you; it's for every believer. In Acts 8:17, "Peter and John placed their hands on them, and they received the Holy Spirit." God often uses Spirit-filled believers to guide and encourage others into this gift.

In Acts 19:6, Paul prayed for new disciples, and "the Holy Spirit came on them, and they spoke in tongues and prophesied." You don't have to be a pastor or leader to help someone receive; you only need faith and willingness.

Galatians 3:14 reminds us that this promise is available to everyone who believes. As you share Scripture, create an atmosphere of expectation, and pray with others, you become a conduit for God's Spirit to move.

Helping others receive deepens your own faith and strengthens the Body of Christ. The same Spirit who filled the early believers is still filling lives today.

Reflection Questions

1. How comfortable are you helping others receive the Spirit's baptism?

____

____

____

2. What Scriptures could you use to guide someone through it?

____

____

____

3. Who in your life might God want you to encourage today?

____

____

____

Secret Place Moment

Pray for boldness and discernment to help someone step deeper into God's promises.

Pray: "Holy Spirit, use me as Your vessel to encourage others and lead them closer to You."

Day 19 — Fanning the Flame

Scripture Focus:

2 Timothy 1:6, Ephesians 5:18, Romans 12:11

Devotional

Paul urged Timothy, "Fan into flame the gift of God, which is in you" (2 Timothy 1:6). Being filled with the Spirit isn't a one-time moment; it's a continual pursuit. Ephesians 5:18 reminds us to "be being filled with the Spirit," staying dependent on His presence daily.

Just like a fire needs tending, your spiritual life needs constant fuel. Prayer, worship, Scripture, and fellowship keep your faith vibrant. Romans 12:11 says, "Never be lacking in zeal, but keep your spiritual fervor, serving the Lord."

Spiritual passion fades when neglected, but when you actively stir your hunger for God, His Spirit fills you afresh. The more you draw near, the more His power flows through you.

Make space today for His fire to be rekindled. God longs to fill you continually so you can shine brightly for Him.

Reflection Questions

1. How would you describe your spiritual passion right now?

2. What practices help you stay filled and refreshed in God's presence?

3. How can you be more intentional about stirring up your hunger for Him?

Secret Place Moment

Set aside time today to worship and invite the Spirit to fill you afresh.

Pray: "Holy Spirit, rekindle the fire within me and keep me burning for You."

Day 20 — Overcoming Opposition

Scripture Focus:

Acts 4:29-31, Matthew 10:19-20, James 1:5

Devotional

Walking in the Spirit doesn't shield you from challenges; it equips you to face them. In Acts 4:29, believers prayed, "Lord, consider their threats and enable Your servants to speak Your word with great boldness." God responded by filling them again with His Spirit, giving courage and strength.

Jesus promised in Matthew 10:19-20, "Do not worry about what to say, for it will not be you speaking, but the Spirit of your Father speaking through you." When you rely on the Spirit, He empowers your words and guides your steps, even in difficult situations.

James 1:5 assures us that God gives wisdom generously when we ask. Opposition becomes an opportunity to demonstrate God's power and faithfulness.

When resistance comes, stay anchored in prayer, trust the Spirit's guidance, and stand firm in God's promises. He has equipped you for victory.

Reflection Questions

1. Where are you facing resistance or spiritual opposition?

___

___

___

2. How can you rely on the Spirit's strength instead of your own?

___

___

___

3. What Scriptures can you stand on for courage?

___

___

___

Secret Place Moment

Ask God to strengthen your heart and fill you with boldness.

Pray: "Holy Spirit, give me courage to face every challenge and wisdom to respond with grace."

Day 21 — It's For Today

Scripture Focus:

Acts 2:39, Hebrews 13:8, John 16:13

Devotional

Peter declared, "The promise is for you and your children and for all who are far off" (Acts 2:39). The baptism, gifts, and power of the Holy Spirit didn't end with the early Church; they are for every believer today.

Hebrews 13:8 says, "Jesus Christ is the same yesterday, today, and forever." If He empowered the apostles, He empowers you. John 16:13 reminds us that the Spirit still guides us into all truth and reveals God's heart.

Secessionism may claim these promises have ceased, but Scripture says otherwise. The Spirit hasn't stopped moving; He's still filling, empowering, and equipping believers to fulfill the Great Commission.

This is your invitation to step deeper into God's power. His promise is alive, active, and available right now. The only question is: will you receive it?

Reflection Questions

1. How does knowing this promise is for today impact your faith?

____

____

____

2. Where do you need to step out and trust God more boldly?

____

____

____

3. How will you live differently, knowing the Spirit empowers you now?

____

____

____

Secret Place Moment

Spend time thanking God for the gift of His Spirit and inviting Him to lead you deeper.

Pray: "Father, thank You that Your promise is for me today. Fill me afresh and empower me to walk fully in Your will."

ABOUT THE AUTHOR

John LoBuglio is a husband, father, pastor, and passionate follower of Jesus. After spending 20 years in the corporate restaurant industry, John encountered God's call to leave the familiar and step into full-time ministry. Today, he serves under Pastor Gary Toney at Victory Life Church in Georgetown, Kentucky, where he helps equip believers to walk in the fullness of God's promises.

Through his own journey of transformation, John has discovered the life-changing reality of living a Spirit-filled life. His desire is to see others awakened to their identity in Christ, empowered by the Holy Spirit, and equipped to fulfill the Great Commission.

His mission is simple: to help believers everywhere experience the promise, power, and presence of the Holy Spirit , because he knows firsthand, it's for today.

www.ingramcontent.com/pod-product-compliance
Lightning Source LLC
LaVergne TN
LVHW010627100826
845148LV00014B/3146

* 9 7 9 8 2 1 8 8 1 3 9 7 0 *